God's Superheroes

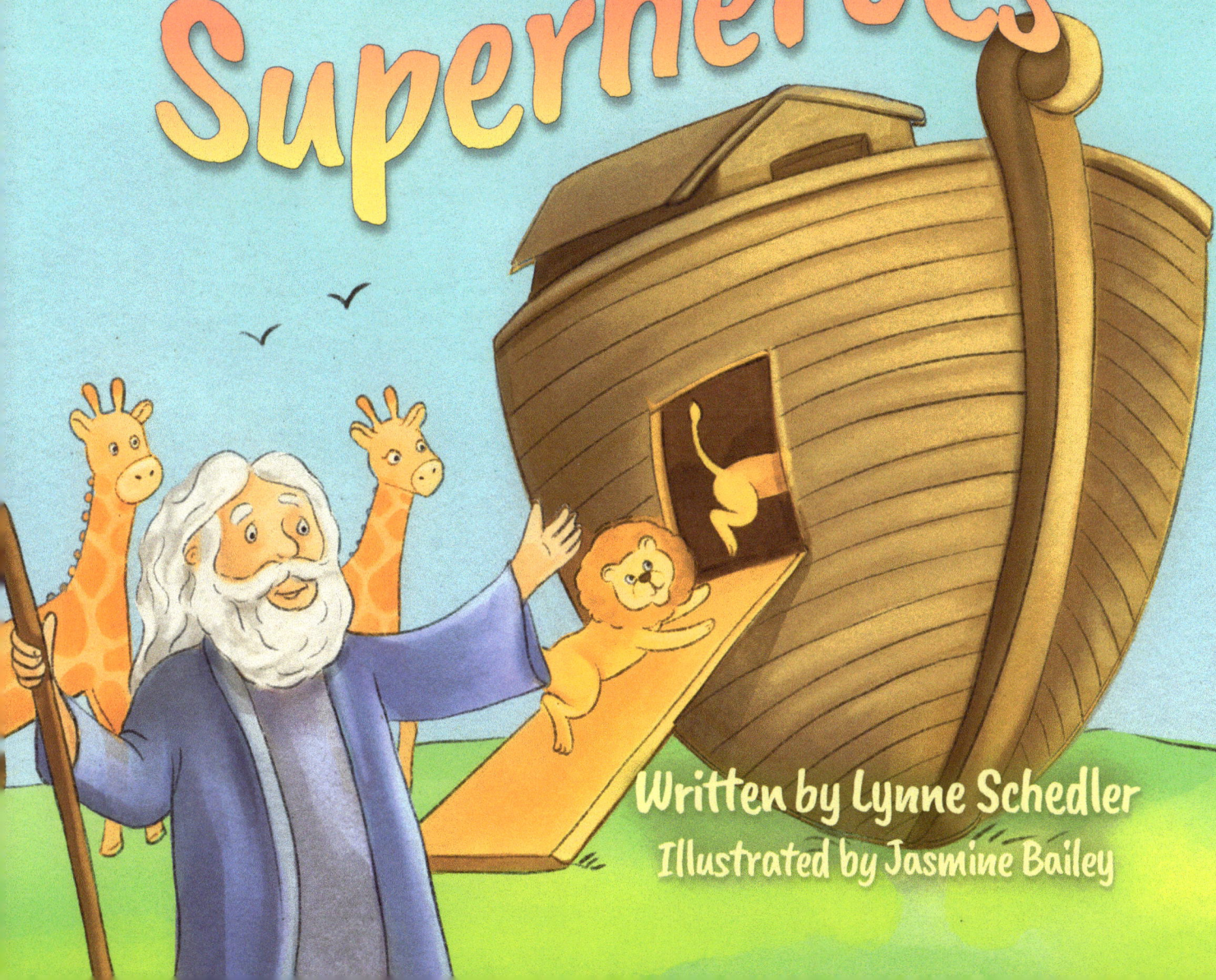

Written by Lynne Schedler

Illustrated by Jasmine Bailey

Hardcover ISBN: 978-1-950685-92-9
Paperback ISBN: 978-1-950685-91-2
Library of Congress: 2022936383

Printed in the United States of America

I dedicate this book to the Lord Jesus Christ; He is the Superhero of all superheroes and the inspiration for all my writing. I hope these stories from the Bible help you realize that you, too, can be one of God's Superheroes.

NOAH, A RIGHTEOUS MAN

Have you ever been asked to do something that was hard? Maybe it seemed impossible, perhaps because you had never done it before, so you didn't know how, or you didn't have the tools you needed for the job.

I bet Noah felt like that too when God told him to build an ark, which is just a really huge boat. The job God asked Noah to do was gigantic! But Noah did not argue with God. He got his family to help, and they began working on the ark. Today, we call it Noah's Ark. It was the length of one and a half football fields and as tall as a seven-story building. The ark took between fifty-five and seventy-five years to build. Remember, Noah did not have the modern tools that we have today.

In the days of Noah, the people on the earth had become very evil all the time, and this grieved God. So, after the ark was finished, God destroyed the earth and everything on it with flood waters. The rain fell for forty days and forty nights, and water covered even the highest mountains on earth by twenty feet. But God saved Noah and his family and some of every kind of living creatures on the earth because Noah was a good man who loved God. God used Noah to carry out His plan to restore the earth again after the flood.

When God looked down and saw man's sin, He wanted to begin again.
People on earth were very bad; it made our God extremely sad.
God saved Noah's house of eight from a world so filled with hate.
An ark he built with God's direction; it was a vessel of perfection.
Their lives were spared from great floodwaters, and they had both sons and daughters.
We all came from Noah's clan; it's all part of God's big plan.

Genesis 6

ABRAHAM, FATHER OF OUR FAITH

Have you ever had to leave your home and go to a new and strange place to live? You might have had to leave your school, your friends, and some of your family behind. Did you think it would be a new and exciting adventure, or did it make you sad and scared? We sometimes don't like changes because we don't know what the new situation is going to be like.

This is probably how Abraham felt when he heard God's voice. God told Abraham to leave his country and his relatives and go to a new country that God would show him. Abraham lived in a big city where false gods were worshiped. God wanted Abraham to cut his ties with the past. God wanted to start a new nation through Abraham and Sarah, his wife. But Abraham would have to move somewhere new; he didn't know where God was leading him, and his family had to live in tents. God told Abraham he was going to make his name very great, and all the nations of the earth would be blessed by him. Abraham did the right thing by believing and obeying God's instructions. He followed God's leading to a new country where he became known as "God's Friend."

Abraham and Sarah didn't have any children, but God promised Abraham that he would have children as countless as the stars in the heavens and as numberless as the grains of sand on the seashore. Abraham believed God, and that is why he is called the "Father of our Faith." Abraham was one hundred years old, and Sarah was around ninety years old when Isaac, the son God promised them, was born. They were definitely senior citizens, but nothing is too hard for our great God. God kept His promise to Abraham. God has greatly blessed his descendants, the Jewish people, and the land of Israel. Christians are part of God's family, too, because of Abraham's faith in God and his obedience to God's command. So we can thank God for Abraham, the "Father of our Faith."

One day, when he heard God's voice, Abraham had to make a choice.
God told him that he must go to a place he did not know.
He packed and left with Sarah his wife; on their journey to a brand-new life.
They left all they knew behind for a land with blessings of every kind.

Genesis 12

JOSEPH, THE DREAMER

What if you got the idea to start a lawn mowing business in your neighborhood? When you told your older brothers, they poked fun at you and said, "That's a dumb idea!" But you knew it was a good idea, and you wondered why they would not encourage you. Wouldn't that make you feel bad? You might think, *Why don't they believe in me and my idea*? Could it be because they did not come up with the idea themselves?

But you went ahead with your plan, and God blessed you. Your business turned out to be an amazing success because your idea came from God.

This is kind of what happened to Joseph. He was his father's favorite son, and this made his brothers jealous. Joseph's father gave him a special colorful coat, and that made his brothers very angry. Joseph had some dreams that he would rule over his brothers and his father and mother. When Joseph told his brothers about his dreams, they hated him even more and planned to kill him. But Joseph's dreams really did come from God; he was speaking about things that would happen in the future. God spoke to Joseph in dreams. Eventually, his dreams promoted him to a position second only to Pharaoh. Joseph's dreams happened. Because God showed Joseph what to do in his dreams, he was able to provide food for his entire family and lots of people during a severe famine throughout Egypt and Canaan.

Joseph was a dreamer,
And he had amazing dreams.
His brothers didn't like him,
So they planned some wicked schemes.
But their plans to kill him,
Only worked for Joseph's good.
They sent him off to Egypt
Where his dreams were understood.
When his dreams were realized,
Then his brothers came to see.
The dreams God gave to Joseph
Blessed their entire family.

Genesis 37, 41–47

MOSES, A DELIVERER

Have you ever seen someone being mistreated, and you wanted to help them? God wants us to help people in trouble, but we must be careful to do it God's way.

One day Moses saw a Hebrew man being beaten by an Egyptian man. Moses was raised in Pharaoh's palace as an Egyptian, but he was really a Hebrew. He was angry that the Egyptian was beating his Hebrew kinsman, so he killed the Egyptian and hid his body in the sand.

The next day Moses saw two Israelites fighting and tried to stop them. But one of them said, "Who made you judge? Are you going to kill me like you killed the Egyptian?" Moses was frightened when he realized people knew what he had done. He ran away from Pharaoh's palace to the desert, where he became a sheepherder.

One day, Moses saw a bush on fire, but it did not burn up. He went closer to see this strange sight, and God spoke to Moses from the bush. God said He would use Moses to free the Israelites from the Egyptians, who mistreated the Israelites horribly.

God gave Moses a special rod to stretch out and perform miracles. One of these miracles was opening the Red Sea, so that the Israelites could escape Pharaoh's pursuing army. After they crossed through the sea on dry ground, the sea closed again and drowned all the Egyptians and their horses. The Israelites rejoiced and praised God for delivering them from the Egyptian army.

Moses came upon a fight.
He desired to make things right.
In anger, he chose wrong instead
By leaving the Egyptian dead.
In fear, he ran away to hide
And in the desert turned aside;
To see a bush that was aflame
And hear God calling out his name.
God guided Moses to set free
His people from captivity.

Exodus 2 and 3

JOSHUA, THE COURAGEOUS

Have you ever had to take someone's place when you felt like you were not able to do as well as the other person did? Perhaps some job was given to you, but you did not feel like you were up to the task.

As an example, let's say you are on the school yearbook staff, and the current editor is leaving. You are asked to take on the job, but you wonder if you can do it well. So much is expected of you, and you do not want to let people down who are counting on you. You want to shine. That very thing happened to Joshua.

Moses led the children of Israel out of slavery in Egypt. He was their leader as they journeyed in the wilderness. But the time came when God wanted Joshua to take over as the new leader of the Israelites. When that happened, Joshua might have felt like he was not up to the task, but the torch of leadership had been passed on to him.

Joshua had been Moses' sidekick for years and had followed in his footsteps. He had learned from the best. Moses was a super leader. So it only makes sense that Joshua might have been a little nervous once the people looked to him for direction. But God knew Joshua was a rock-solid leader; he was up to the task. Joshua ushered God's people into the Promised Land that God had given them. He led them to victory over their enemies because he was courageous and looked to God to lead him.

Joshua missed his leader after Moses died.
He'd been right there with him faithfully by his side.
The people looked to him; as they marched, he led.
So he could not look back; he had to look ahead.
Six days they circled Jericho, marching hushed around the wall.
The seventh day the trumpet's blast and shouts caused it to fall.
Many battles Joshua faced all along the way.
But God gave him the victory at the end of the day.

Joshua 1, 6

GIDEON, THE FAINTHEARTED

Have you ever felt like you are not as capable as other people? Maybe you are from a one-parent family, and you have not had the same advantages as some other kids. You might feel that you lack experience. Even when you do not feel confident in your ability, God will give you the ability to do whatever He asks you to do. Rely on God's ability, not yours. You can do all things through Christ who strengthens you.

The Israelites did evil in the Lord's eyes by worshiping foreign gods. When they turned away from the Lord, the Midianites ruled over them. They invaded their land and plundered their crops and livestock. The Israelites made shelters in caves and cried to the Lord for help, and the Lord sent an angel to a man named Gideon. The angel told Gideon that God would use him to deliver Israel from the Midianites.

Gideon wondered how he could do this, since he was from a poor family in the weakest tribe. But the Lord said, "I will be with you, and you will strike down all the Midianites."

Gideon demolished the altar of the false god Baal and built an altar to the Lord. He rallied the troops to go after the Midianites. God had a unique way of choosing the best men to fight with Gideon. First, God told Gideon to send all fearful men home. Twenty-two thousand left, but Gideon still had ten thousand men ready to fight. God told Gideon he still had too many soldiers, and he should send home those who bowed down on their knees to drink from the brook. Gideon was allowed to keep the three hundred men who lapped up water from their hands like dogs. How would you like to start into battle with thirty-two thousand soldiers and then have God send away all but the three hundred?

Gideon gave these men trumpets and jars with lamps inside. He divided them into three groups, and they descended on the Midian camp. They blew their trumpets, smashed the jars, and held the lamps while shouting, "The sword of the Lord and of Gideon." In confusion, the enemy lashed out at each other with their swords and ran. The Israelites hunted down the Midianites that got away. God used a simple man to defeat the enemy and free the Israelites from harsh treatment. Then they lived peacefully for forty years, and Gideon died at a very old age.

Gideon was a simple man not trained in how to fight.
God used him to get victory for the Israelites.
They came upon the Midian camp and caught them unaware.
They blew trumpets and broke jars to show that they were there.
"The sword of the Lord and of Gideon!" This was their battle cry.
Turning swords upon their friends, the foe began to die.
Some of them ran for their lives from the army of the Lord.
They feared the worst was yet to come, and they died by the sword.
Gideon saw the battle won, for God had lent a hand.
There was peace for forty years, all throughout the land.

Judges 6–8

SAMSON, THE STRONG

Do you know how important it is to pick your friends carefully? I am sure you have heard the expression, "One bad apple spoils the whole bunch." This is especially true when it comes to bad company. Pick the kind of friends that you want to be like. Listen to your parents; they have experience in judging character. This is extremely important when you start dating. God wants you to pick friends with high moral standards.

Samson the Nazirite failed at this. To show their devotion to God, Nazirites were to follow some special rules. For example, they were not to drink wine or strong drink or cut their hair. God gave Samson a gift of extraordinary strength. He killed a lion with his bare hands and wiped out one thousand Philistines with a donkey's jawbone. But Samson chose the wrong girlfriend. His parents warned him, but he didn't listen. Samson fell in love with Delilah, a Philistine. She pestered him for the secret of what made him so strong. Finally, he gave in and told her it was his long hair.

When Samson fell asleep with his head on her lap, she had a servant shave his head. Samson's strength was gone. His captors poked out his eyes and threw him in prison. While he labored in prison, Samson begged God for one chance to avenge himself against the Philistines. His captors didn't notice that Sampson's hair grew long again while he was in prison.

One day, blind Samson was taken to a celebration where the Philistines planned to make fun of him. As he stood between the pillars that held up the temple, Samson asked God to use him once again to defeat the Philistines. He pushed on the pillars with all his might, and God gave him strength one last time. The pillars fell, and the temple collapsed. Everyone in the building died, including Samson. He killed more Philistines at his death than he had killed in his whole life.

Samson was a mighty man,
For God had made him strong.
He loved the shrewd Delilah,
But for him she was all wrong.
She pestered him to tell her
Where he got his strength.
Finally, he told her
From his hair and from its length.
As he slept upon her lap,
A servant cut his hair.
Then, he wakened from his nap;
His strength no longer there.
His captors, they made fun of him
And poked out both his eyes.
His strength returned to him again
And that was their demise.
The pillars gave way
When he pushed;
The temple, it did fall.
Though Samson sadly met his death,
The Philistines? He killed them all.

Judges 16

RUTH, THE LOYAL

Have you ever had a time in your life when you had to make a really important decision—a life-changing decision? At some point in our lives, we all must make decisions like this. We must decide whether we will go forward into the unknown or cling to the security of what we know. We must pray and ask the Lord for wisdom and guidance. The Bible says that God directs our footsteps, and He will guide us if we trust Him.

Ruth, a Moabitess, faced just such a situation. Tragedy had struck her family. Her Israelite husband, her father-in-law, and her brother-in-law had all died. All the men in her family were gone, and being a widow in that day was awfully hard. She could not just go out and get a job. Her mother-in-law, Naomi, decided to go back to her home in Bethlehem. Naomi told Ruth to stay in Moab and return to her mother's house, but Ruth loved Naomi so she would not stay.

Ruth clung to Naomi and promised to go with her wherever she went, and that Naomi's God would be her God too. Ruth was loyal to her husband's mother. Loyalty is an outstanding quality and one that pleases God.

When her husband passed away, her future Ruth didn't know.
She clung to Naomi's side and went where she did go.
They returned to Bethlehem, known as "The House of Bread."
Ruth picked grain from stranger's fields, so that they could be fed.
Ruth found favor with her God and met a wealthy man.

Boaz was this rich man's name;
He was part of God's plan.
Boaz fell in love with Ruth
And took her for his wife.
So they lived in Bethlehem;
Ruth had a brand-new life.
Ruth and Boaz had a boy;
Naomi cared for him.
They all found
Such peace and joy
Right there in Bethlehem.

The Book of Ruth

DAVID, THE GIANT KILLER

Do you have any bullies at your school? Most all schools have at least one. They are loud, and they throw their weight around by making threats. They control people by making them afraid. Bullies are insecure, and they make up for it by pushing people around. Most of the time, they pick on kids smaller than they are. If someone challenges them, they will usually back down.

David encountered one of these bullies when he was running an errand for his father, delivering bread and cheeses to his older brothers who served in King Saul's army. At that time, the Israelites were holed up in the valley of Elah. Only the valley stood between them and the Philistines.

For forty days, Goliath, the Philistine hero, came out twice a day and taunted the Israelites. Goliath was almost ten feet tall, and the Israelites were terrified of him. When David saw what was happening, he asked what would be done for the man who killed Goliath. He was told that man would be rewarded with King Saul's daughter's hand in marriage, great wealth, and his family's taxes would be canceled. When David's brother overheard his questions, he became extremely angry. He made fun of David. "Who's watching over your flocks?" he snarled.

David had a fearless spirit, and he vowed to kill Goliath. King Saul sent for David and offered him his armor, but it was not the right size for David, so he would not wear it. Armed with only his sling and five smooth stones, David approached Goliath. Goliath cursed him, insulted and angry that the Israelites would send a youth to fight him. David ran toward Goliath in the name of the Lord, and he brought the giant down with just one stone. Then he took Goliath's sword and lopped off his head. The Philistines ran for the hills. Shouts of victory were heard in the Israelite camp, and David became a superhero to the Israelites on that day.

David was a shepherd boy; he watched the sheep with care.
Once he killed, with his own hands, a lion and a bear.
When David faced off with Goliath,
He went out in the name of the Lord.
He felled the giant with one smooth stone;
Then he took his head off with his sword.
God had much greater things for him;
David had a higher call.
He became a champion strong
And the king who replaced Saul.

1 Samuel 17

NEHEMIAH, THE BUILDER

How would you feel if your house caught on fire and burned to the ground, and everything was gone? Or what if your hometown was destroyed by wildfires? I am sure you would be overcome with sadness and would probably cry. If you moved away, you would wonder how the people were doing who still lived there. You might even want to go back and help them rebuild the town.

That is probably how Nehemiah felt when he heard that Jerusalem, his beloved city, was in ruins. The walls were broken down, and the gates to the city had been burned. Nehemiah was living in another country, but his heart was broken when he heard the news. He wanted to return and help rebuild the city walls. In those days, cities had walls around them for protection.

Nehemiah asked King Artaxerxes for permission to take leave of his job and go back to Jerusalem. The king granted his request and gave Nehemiah letters to ensure his safe travel and to help him get timber to use for the walls. The job ahead of him was huge. The entire time Nehemiah and his workers repaired the wall, they were harassed by the enemy; but Nehemiah did not quit. God helped him finish the project in fifty-two days. When the job was done, they dedicated their work and celebrated. God's Word was read, and the people confessed their sin so Jerusalem could be completely restored.

Nehemiah wept, to hear the city gates were burned.
He got permission from the king to grant him a return.
On his heart, his God had placed a very special call.
He wanted to go back home and help rebuild the wall.
The job was very difficult; foes tried to make him stop.
But Nehemiah wouldn't quit until he reached the top.
God's law was read to everyone, and all confessed their sin.
Then, all the people did rejoice. The wall was built again!

Nehemiah 1–9

ESTHER, THE QUEEN

Have you ever been at just the right place at just the right time? Maybe it was when you were looking for a bike or a dog or you met someone new and became best friends; that is called favor. God has a plan, and He knows just the right people to carry out His plan. Nothing satisfies you more than knowing God is using you to accomplish His plan. We are the only hands, feet, voice, and heartbeat God has here on earth. We are the instruments God chooses to use.

Esther was not always the queen. Her cousin, Mordecai, raised her after the death of her parents. King Ahasuerus threw a big party and invited many important guests. He called for Queen Vashti to show everyone how beautiful she was, but she refused to come. The king was furious and vowed to reject her as queen because she had publicly dishonored him.

He organized a search for beautiful girls to add to his harem; one of these girls would replace the queen. He was very pleased with Esther and placed the crown on her. God promoted Esther to queen. King Ahasuerus did not know Esther was Jewish because Mordecai had told her not to reveal her heritage.

The king honored Haman, a high official, by commanding all the other officials to bow down to him. Mordecai refused to bow, and this enraged Haman. Haman looked for a way to destroy Mordecai and his people. God used Queen Esther to keep the Jewish people from being destroyed. She came to be queen for such a time as this.

Esther was chosen to be queen,
Though it was unexpected.
When you choose to serve our God,
You will be connected.
Haman hatched an evil plot
To rid the land of Jews.
It never ever crossed his mind,
"Queen Esther's Jewish too."
When the king learned Haman's plan,
It backfired on him.
Haman hung from gallows high
Where Mordecai would've been.

The Book of Esther

DANIEL, THE DEVOTED

Have you ever been in a situation where someone wanted you to do something wrong? Maybe they wanted you to tell a lie for them or give them your homework. It takes integrity to say no and do what you know is right when people put pressure on you. But your conscience tells you what is right and what is wrong.

This is what happened to Daniel. Some government leaders did not like Daniel because the king was planning to put him in charge of the whole kingdom. So these leaders tricked King Darius into passing an unchangeable law that commanded people to pray only to the king for thirty days. Whoever broke this law would be thrown into the lion's den. These evil men knew that Daniel would not pray to the king, so they thought they could get rid of him this way.

Daniel was devoted, so he kept on praying to God before an open window facing Jerusalem, as he always did. He was arrested and thrown into the lion's den because he had broken the king's law. But God sent an angel to lock the mouths of the lions so they could not hurt Daniel. When the king learned that God had protected Daniel from the lions, he rejoiced and threw those evil men into the lion's den, and the lions devoured them.

Daniel was a man of God
Who prayed three times a day.
When the law said he must stop,
He chose not to obey.
They threw him in the lion's den;
They'd eat him up alive.
An angel locked the lion's mouths,
And Daniel did survive. When the king learned of this plan,
His foes went in the den.
The lions there were ravenous;
They quickly ate the men.

Daniel 6

MARY, MOTHER OF THE MESSIAH

Have you ever had to do something that you knew the Lord was telling you to do, but you knew in your heart that people would not understand? They might misjudge you or accuse you of being insensitive. Maybe God told you to break off a friendship with someone because He knew that relationship would only hurt you. People look on outward actions, but God looks on the heart. He knows if you want to please and follow Him.

Mary was a young woman engaged to marry Joseph, a carpenter in her hometown. She was probably making wedding plans and was excited about their approaching wedding day. Then something miraculous happened that changed the course of history. History would be decided by Mary's response. An angel appeared to Mary and told her that God had chosen her to be the Messiah's mother. She was confused and did not understand how that could happen, but she humbly accepted the angel's announcement by saying, "Be it unto me according to thy word."

Mary was a humble girl, a servant of the Lord.
So when the angel came to her she listened to His word.
"God has chosen you to be the mother of His Son.
You've been so highly favored by the Holy One."
Mary's heart was troubled; she didn't understand.
"How can this be?" she wondered. "I haven't known a man."
"The Holy Spirit, He will come
And overshadow you.
Elizabeth, your cousin dear,
Is having a child too.
Your baby, Jesus is His name,
The Savior and your Lord."
She said, "Let it be done to me,
According to your word."

Luke 1

JONAH, THE EVANGELIST

Have you ever been told to do something that you really did not want to do, so you did something else instead, thinking it would be okay? Maybe you felt the Lord prompting you to share about Jesus with some kids at school. But you thought they might reject or make fun of you, so you chose to go hang out with your friends instead. As a result, you will never know how God could have used you to touch the hearts of kids who did not know Him. Sometimes we do not get a second chance, so that's why it is important to listen and obey the Holy Spirit's voice.

God told Jonah to go to a very large city called Nineveh. The people in Nineveh did not know God and were living wickedly. Because of their awful sin, God was going to destroy Nineveh. But God loves people, so He gave them a chance to change. God told Jonah to tell the people to turn from their sin to the living God. If they would not, after forty days, their city and everything within its walls would be destroyed.

Jonah did not want to go to Nineveh, so he boarded a ship going to Tarshish instead. After the ship launched out to sea, a violent storm arose, and everyone's life was in danger. The crew tried to save the ship by throwing cargo overboard and by praying to their gods. Jonah was asleep below deck when the captain came to him and asked how he could sleep in such a violent storm. Jonah admitted the storm came because he was running from God. He told them to throw him overboard and the storm would cease. When the crew threw Jonah into the sea, the storm stopped at once.

Jonah sank into the depths of the sea, but God had prepared a great fish to swallow him. Jonah was in the fish's belly for three days and three nights. While he was there, Jonah prayed and repented for disobeying God. Finally, the fish vomited Jonah out onto the dry land. Again, God told Jonah to go and warn the people of Nineveh. This time Jonah obeyed God and set out for Nineveh to warn the people of the coming destruction. The king called on all the people to fast and turn to God, so the people repented.

Jonah became truly angry when the people in Nineveh repented because they were enemies of his nation. In other words, he obeyed God and delivered the warning, but he really wanted God to destroy them. He went outside the city and sat down to watch what would happen to the people of Nineveh. It was extremely hot, so God caused a plant to grow that shaded him from the scorching sun. Jonah was grateful for the plant, but the next morning God prepared a worm that killed the gourd. Jonah became angry because the plant died. God asked him why he was angry about a plant dying, yet he had no concern for the hundreds of thousands of people in Nineveh that would have perished if they had not turned to God.

God had a word for Nineveh—
"Jonah, go without delay.
Unless they turn from their sin,
I'll destroy them in forty days."
Jonah disobeyed the Lord;
To Tarshish he sailed instead.
Caught up in a violent storm,
He almost wound up dead.
He took the blame for the storm.
He was running from the Lord.
So, to calm the raging sea,
they tossed him overboard.
Jonah sank into the depths.
His plight was looking grim.
But God prepared a great big fish
To come and swallow him.

In its belly, Jonah prayed.
He was spewed out on the beach.
Then, he went to Nineveh,
Where he began to preach.
In Nineveh, old Jonah spoke
The message from the Lord.
The people, saddened by their sin,
Did listen to his words.
Jonah got angry and he said,
"I knew this from the start!"
God rebuked him for his wrath
And the hardness of his heart.
God said, "You cared more for the plant
I gave to you for shade,
Than for the folks in Nineveh
Who listened and obeyed."

The Book of Jonah

JESUS, THE MESSIAH

Have you ever felt like no one really understood you? Maybe you were having a hard time in school with a certain subject. Perhaps you felt like you just didn't fit into a circle of friends. It could be that you lost someone you loved dearly, and you were really sad. The Bible tells us that Jesus went through the same things we go through, and He knows how we feel. He wants us to turn to Him for help.

Jesus came from heaven to earth on a special assignment. He was born as a baby, just like you, and He grew up as a child and teenager, just like you. He worked with His earthly dad in his carpentry shop and learned a trade. He went to temple, just like we go to church, and He listened to the teachers. He knew when He came into this world that He would have to die on the cross for our sins. Someone had to do it, and He's the only one who could, since He never sinned. But Jesus experienced the same things we do. He was sad when His own people rejected Him. He was happy when He turned the water into wine for the wedding guests in Cana. He became angry when He saw the temple being used like a market instead of a house for prayer. He was betrayed by His friends at the time He needed them most. He knew what it felt like to be all alone.

Jesus is the Superhero of all God's Superheroes. He performed many miracles, like healing the blind man, the crippled man, the man with a paralyzed hand, the men with leprosy, and the woman who hemorrhaged.

He helped a man who was battling demons and cutting himself. He even brought dead people back to life. He fed five thousand people with just five loaves of bread and two fishes by blessing a little boy's lunch. He walked on the water to His disciples. He spoke to the wind and waves and calmed the storm. Jesus healed all who came to Him, and He forgave sinners of their sins. He told them how much His Heavenly Father loved them. The wonderful thing is that He is still doing the same things today. He gave His disciples power to do the same things He did. He gives us that power too, if we will obey the Holy Spirit's voice and ask Him to come into our heart. Jesus loves you, and He wants to work through you to bless others. May God bless and help you to become a superhero for God.

Jesus is our Superhero;
He's the very best!
Out of all the superheroes,
He outshines the rest!
He came to earth from Heaven
To show us how to live,
To walk with God and fellowman,
To love us and forgive.

Do you want to know God's secret?
Love's His secret power!
The Holy Spirit is your helper
In this day and hour.
Want to be a superhero
God uses every day?
Make Jesus the King of your heart,
And He'll show you the way.

The Gospels of Matthew, Mark,
Luke, and John

PAUL, THE APOSTLE

Have you ever thought you were one hundred percent right about something? Then later you found out that you were wrong, and people had been hurt by your actions. A lot of times, angry words have been spoken. Perhaps you felt deeply sorry afterward, and you changed your mind. When this happens, we should go to the person we have hurt, tell them we were wrong, and ask their forgiveness. We do not need to have an experience like Paul to show us we have been wrong. The Holy Spirit will correct us with God's Word.

The Apostle Paul was quite a character. He was a very devoted Jewish man, and he hated the followers of Jesus. He gave orders for Christians to be arrested, dragging them from their homes and throwing them in prison. During this entire time, Paul thought his actions were unquestionably right, and he was doing God a favor.

But one day, Paul had a face-to-face encounter with Jesus. A bright light from heaven shined down on him. Paul was blinded by the light and fell to the ground. Jesus called Paul by name and asked him why he was persecuting Him. Paul didn't know that when he hurt Christians, he was hurting God.

God had a special mission for Paul. He wanted Paul to preach the good news of salvation through Jesus Christ to people who were not Jewish. Paul started many churches in his travels. He visited them more than once and wrote them letters. Paul's letters are in the Bible. He wrote over half of the New Testament. At the end of his life, Paul was under house arrest by the Roman government. Paul was one of the most powerful Christians in the early Church. He was just as strong in his devotion to living for Jesus, as he was a Jewish man devoted to keeping God's law.

Traveling down Damascus Road,
Paul met Jesus one day.
The light he saw was so bright
It took his sight away. Jesus asked, "Paul,
Why are you persecuting Me?"
From that day on,
Paul embraced Christianity.
God designed a special task
That He chose Paul to do:
Take the gospel to the Gentiles
Even though you're a Jew.
All would know that Paul had changed,
And God would get the glory.
This is how God had arranged
To spread the gospel story.

Acts 9

GOD'S SUPERHERO

Now that you have read the accounts of these superheroes, why don't you imagine yourself as one of God's Superheroes too? God's Superheroes are needed just as much today as they were in the past, and maybe even more. God wants to use YOU to work His mighty miracles in our world today. So write your name on the line and put your picture in the frame. Place it where you will see it every day (like on the bathroom mirror or refrigerator). When you see your picture, say, "I'm one of God's Superheroes; He is working His mighty works through me."

"Truly, truly I say to you, the one who believes in Me, the works that I do, he will do also; and greater works than these he will do; because I am going to the Father" (John 14:12, NASB).

The superheroes you have read about are just a few of many found in the pages of the Bible. I hope you will be inspired to read more remarkable stories about the people that God used. There is no expiration date on God's Word; these examples still apply for us today. God bless you!

_____

Put your picture in this frame,
And on the line write your name.
"Jesus, this is what I pray;
Use me each and every day.
I want to be like those of old.
Make me Lord both strong and bold."
See what great things God will do,
When you let Him work through you.

Would you like to meet these real superheroes someday?

They're all in heaven waiting to meet you and tell you about their real-life adventures. If you would like to go to heaven someday, God tells us in the Bible how to get there.

- The Bible tells us that we are all sinners. "For all have sinned and fall short of God's glory" (Romans 3:23). Sin is the wrong things we do (like telling a lie or stealing, or fighting, or refusing to obey). Have you sinned?

- The Bible tells us there is a penalty or payment required for our sin. Think about someone who does something wrong and is caught by the police. That person must pay a fine or maybe even to go to jail for their wrongdoing. In the same way, we can't go to heaven unless someone pays the penalty for our sin. "For the wages of sin is death" (Romans 6:23). If we don't choose to follow Jesus in this life, we will not get to live with Him in heaven when we die. But God loves us so much that He has made a way for us to go to heaven by accepting Jesus' death on the cross as payment for our sin and by asking Him into our hearts.

- The Bible also tells us that we can't pay for our own sin. We must accept that Jesus paid our sin debt. God loves us so much that He wants us to be in heaven with Him. God gave His Son Jesus, Who never sinned, to die on the cross to pay for our sins so that we can go to heaven someday. That's God's gift to us, and it is a gift that is completely paid for. If someone gives you a gift, do you have to pay for it? No. You simply accept the gift and thank them. God's gift is the same way. We can have the gift of heaven if we will simply ask for it.

- The Bible tells us in Romans 10:13 that if we call on the Lord and ask Him to save us, He will: "For 'everyone who calls on the name of the Lord will be saved.'" Once you accept God's gift of forgiveness for your sins, you have His promise that He will never leave you, and that you can always know for sure that you have a home in heaven someday (Hebrews 13:5 and 1 John 5:13). Pray this simple prayer if you would like to accept Jesus as your Savior and go to heaven:

Dear God, I believe Jesus is Your Son, and that He died on the cross to pay for my sin. I confess that I have sinned, and I need Jesus to forgive me and come into my heart and be my Savior. I accept your gift of salvation now. Jesus, I know that you are preparing a home for me in heaven, and I will come to heaven one day and live with You and God my Father and the Holy Spirit. Thank you, Jesus, Amen.

MEET THE AUTHOR

Lynne Schedler is a wife, mother, and grandmother who lives in Florida with her family. Lynne grew up in Kansas City, Kansas, and moved with her family to Louisiana during her senior year of high school. There she met and married Richard, her husband of fifty-three years. They have one son and one grandson, who is twenty.

Lynne loves animals; she and Richard have two Rat Terriers, Bolt and Chili, who are very special family members. Lynne gave her life to Jesus as a child in Bible school. She loves to write, especially poetry, and she also enjoys interior decorating.

Lynne Schedler is also the author of the whimsical children's book *What Is Heaven Really Like*? This title is available for sale on Amazon, Barnes & Noble, and other book retail sites. For bulk sales or events, please contact the author at Lschedler@cfl.rr.com.

www.ingramcontent.com/pod-product-compliance
Lightning Source LLC
LaVergne TN
LVHW070835080426

835508LV00031B/3465